IN THE WEB WE TRUST

The importance and usefulness of websites

Brain Jose
Webber Knowsbest

DESCRIPTION

"In Web We Trust: Unveiling the Power of Online Resources" Discover the pivotal role that thousands of websites play in shaping our lives, from information access to communication, and explore the trust we invest in these virtual portals to navigate the vast digital landscape.

"In Web We Trust: Unraveling the Significance of Online Platforms" Embark on an enlightening journey through the significance of thousands of websites that serve as gateways to knowledge, commerce, and social connections, delving into the profound impact they have on modern society.

"In Web We Trust: Unleashing the Potential of a Digital Ecosystem" Uncover the untapped potential of the digital world as we delve into the pivotal role thousands of websites play in creating a thriving interconnected ecosystem, fostering innovation and transformation.

"In Web We Trust: Empowering Humanity through Virtual Empires" Dive into the empowering world of thousands of websites, and witness how these virtual empires have become indispensable tools for personal and professional growth, revolutionizing the way we live and work.

"In Web We Trust: Navigating the Digital Ocean of Websites" Embark on a captivating exploration of the vast digital ocean and its myriad websites, illuminating how trust in these online platforms influences our decisions and shapes the very fabric of our daily lives.

"In Web We Trust: The Internet's Endless Tapestry of Knowledge" Journey through the intricate tapestry of knowledge woven by thousands of websites, and comprehend how the trust we place in these digital threads enriches our understanding of the world.

"In Web We Trust: Embracing the Web's Ever-Expanding Horizons" Embrace the boundless horizons of the web as we unveil the multitude of websites that have become indispensable companions in our pursuit of growth, learning, and meaningful connections.

"In Web We Trust: The Digital Revolution's Unbreakable Bonds" Explore the unbreakable bonds between individuals, businesses, and knowledge through the lens of thousands of websites, illuminating how our collective trust fuels the digital revolution.

"In Web We Trust: The Renaissance of Human Interaction in Cyberspace" Unravel the renaissance of human interaction facilitated by thousands of websites, revolutionizing communication, collaboration, and the way we build trust in the digital realm.

"In Web We Trust: The Online Odyssey of Reliability and Utility" Embark on an extraordinary odyssey through the online world, where the reliability and utility of thousands of websites take center stage, shaping our modern reality and igniting a new era of digital trust.

The table of contents

1... ANSWERTHEPUBLIC.COM

AnswerThePublic.com is a useful online tool for keyword and content research, particularly for content creators, digital marketers, and SEO professionals. It works by generating visualizations of search data from Google and Bing, presenting it in the form of questions, prepositions, and related terms that people frequently search for on the internet. Here are some ways in which the site can be beneficial:

Content Ideation: AnswerThePublic.com helps content creators come up with fresh and relevant ideas for blog posts, articles, videos, and other types of content. By understanding what questions and topics are trending in their niche, they can tailor their content to meet the specific needs of their target audience.

SEO and Keyword Research: The tool provides insights into the specific phrases and questions that users are using to search for information. This information is valuable for optimizing website content and improving its visibility in search engine results pages (SERPs).

Understanding User Intent: By analyzing the questions and terms that users are searching for, businesses can gain a better understanding of user intent. This allows them to create content that aligns with what users are looking for, leading to more relevant and engaging interactions.

Competitive Analysis: AnswerThePublic.com can also be used to analyze the questions and topics that competitors are targeting. This information can help businesses identify content gaps and opportunities to differentiate themselves in the market.

Social Media and Content Promotion: The insights from the tool can be used to shape social media strategies and promotions. Knowing what topics are trending can guide businesses in creating shareable and relevant content for their social media channels.

Blogging and Q&A Sections: The tool can provide inspiration for blog post titles and help identify frequently asked questions that can be addressed in a website's Q&A section, improving the overall user experience.

It's worth noting that the usefulness of AnswerThePublic.com may vary depending on the specific needs and goals of individual users. Additionally, since the internet landscape is constantly evolving, it's a good idea to explore other tools and resources for keyword and content research to ensure comprehensive insights.

It has about 200+ templates and bring your ideas to life with high-quality content.
Parts of its usefulness includes
Elevate your YouTube videos with Cohesive's AI script generator
Exploring the Evolution of AI Image Generator
Full Blog Generator Fabulously easy - whip up an SEO-friendly blog for traffic
Instagram Caption: Create a catchy caption for your Instagram post
Content Rephrase : Express your content in a different way
Facebook Post : Write an engaging Facebook post about a topic
Story Generator: Keep your audience engaged with a fascinating story
LinkedIn Post: Compose a catchy post for LinkedIn
Script for TikTok Video: Generate scripts that engage your audience

Its uses
Marketing
Sales
Support
Personal

Its features include
AI editor
AI Voices
Templates
Inspiration

Its templates includes
Sales
Social Media
Writing Assistant
Marketing
Product Management
HR Management
Legal
Education
Formal Writing
Business
General
Training Material

3...Pexels.com

Pexels.com is a popular and highly useful website that offers a vast collection of high-quality, free stock photos and videos. Its primary purpose is to provide content creators, designers, marketers, and anyone in need of visual assets with a valuable resource. Here are some of the key reasons why Pexels.com is considered useful:

Extensive Library: Pexels.com boasts a massive library of free stock photos and videos contributed by a community of talented photographers and videographers. With thousands of new images and videos added regularly, users have a wide variety of options to choose from for their projects.

High Quality: The platform is known for curating high-quality content, ensuring that the images and videos available are visually appealing and meet professional standards.

Free and Easy to Use: All the assets on Pexels.com are available for free, and users can download and use them without any attribution requirements in most cases. This convenience makes it a popular choice for those who need visuals without the hassle of licensing or fees.

Versatility: Pexels.com covers a broad range of topics and themes, making it suitable for various purposes. Whether it's for website design, blog posts, social media, presentations, or marketing campaigns, users can find relevant visuals to complement their content.

Search and Discovery: The website offers robust search functionality, allowing users to find specific images or videos based on keywords and tags. Additionally, Pexels.com has a discovery feature that suggests related images, which can be helpful for finding alternative options or complementary visuals.

API Integration: Pexels.com provides an API (Application Programming Interface) that developers can integrate into their applications and platforms. This enables seamless access to the platform's vast collection of visuals directly from within other tools.

Curated Collections: Pexels.com organizes its content into curated collections, making it easier for users to explore and find images and videos that fit specific themes or moods.

User-Friendly Licensing: Pexels.com uses the Creative Commons Zero (CC0) license for most of its content. This license allows users to modify, copy, and distribute the assets without asking for permission, even for commercial purposes.

Overall, Pexels.com is a valuable resource for anyone in need of high-quality visual content without the burden of cost or complex licensing requirements. However, it's essential to note that platforms may change over time, so it's a good idea to check the latest information.

4... Veed.io

Veed.io is an online video editing platform that provides various tools and features to edit and enhance videos easily. While I don't have access to real-time information, I can share some of the general usefulness of Veed.io based on its features up to my last update:

> User-Friendly Video Editing: Veed.io is designed to be user-friendly, making it accessible to individuals with various levels of video editing experience. Its intuitive interface allows users to trim, cut, merge, and add text and images to their videos without the need for complex software.
>
> Cloud-Based Platform: As a cloud-based video editor, Veed.io does not require any downloads or installations. Users can access the platform from any device with an internet connection, allowing for flexibility and convenience in video editing tasks.
>
> Support for Various Video Formats: Veed.io supports a wide range of video formats, enabling users to upload and edit videos in different file types without worrying about compatibility issues.
>
> Text and Captioning: The platform offers tools to add text, captions, and subtitles to videos. This feature is beneficial for content creators who want to make their videos more accessible and engaging for a broader audience.
>
> Filters and Effects: Veed.io provides filters and effects that users can apply to their videos to enhance the visual appeal and overall quality.
>
> Video Speed Control: Users can adjust the speed of their videos, allowing them to create time-lapse or slow-motion effects.
>
> Audio Editing: Veed.io allows users to edit and manipulate audio tracks, which is essential for ensuring the audio quality matches the video content.
>
> Social Media Optimization: The platform provides predefined aspect ratios suitable for various social media platforms, making it easier for users to create videos optimized for specific channels.
>
> Collaboration Features: Veed.io offers collaboration capabilities, allowing multiple users to work together on the same video project simultaneously.
>
> Video Export and Sharing: Once the editing is complete, users can export the edited video in different resolutions and formats. They can also directly share the video on various social media platforms from within the platform.

Keep in mind that the features and usefulness of Veed.io may evolve over time, and new functionalities might have been added since my last update. It's always a good idea to visit the Veed.io website directly to explore the most up-to-date information on its features, pricing, and services.

5... Elsaspeaks.com

Elsa Speak (also known as ELSA) is a language learning app and website designed to help non-native English speakers improve their pronunciation and speaking skills. It stands for "English Language Speech Assistant." Here are some key points about the potential usefulness of Elsa Speak:

Pronunciation Improvement: One of the primary purposes of Elsa Speak is to assist language learners in improving their English pronunciation. The app uses speech recognition technology to analyze users' pronunciation and provides instant feedback and corrections, helping them sound more natural and fluent.

Personalized Learning: Elsa Speak uses artificial intelligence algorithms to adapt to individual learners' needs. The app offers personalized lessons and exercises based on the user's pronunciation strengths and weaknesses, ensuring targeted practice.

Accent Reduction: For those who wish to reduce their accent and sound more like native English speakers, Elsa Speak can be particularly valuable. The app focuses on teaching the pronunciation and intonation patterns commonly found in American English.

Convenience and Flexibility: As a mobile app and web platform, Elsa Speak offers learners the flexibility to practice English pronunciation at their convenience. Learners can use the app on their smartphones or access it through a web browser.

Real-Life Context: The app provides pronunciation practice within real-life conversational contexts, allowing learners to apply their newly acquired skills in everyday situations.

Progress Tracking: Elsa Speak offers progress tracking features that allow learners to monitor their improvement over time. This can be motivating and helps learners stay committed to their language learning goals.

Vocabulary and Phrases: The app not only focuses on pronunciation but also includes vocabulary and common phrases used in everyday English conversations, providing a holistic learning experience.

Suitable for Various Proficiency Levels: Elsa Speak is designed to accommodate learners of different proficiency levels, from beginners to advanced learners, making it accessible to a wide range of users.

It's important to note that the usefulness of Elsa Speak or any language learning tool depends on individual learning styles, preferences, and goals. Additionally, as technology and apps continue to evolve, there may have been updates or changes to Elsa Speak since my last update. For the latest information about Elsa Speak and its features, it's best to visit the official website or app store listings.

6... Ifixit.com

iFixit.com is a highly useful website that provides comprehensive repair guides and resources for a wide range of electronic devices, gadgets, and appliances. The site's primary focus is on empowering users to repair their devices themselves, promoting the principles of repairability, sustainability, and reducing electronic waste. Here are some key points highlighting the usefulness of iFixit.com:

Repair Guides and Manuals: iFixit offers detailed step-by-step repair guides, teardowns, and service manuals for a vast array of electronic devices, including smartphones, laptops, tablets, game consoles, cameras, and household appliances. These guides provide invaluable assistance to users who want to fix their devices instead of replacing them or seeking costly professional repairs.

DIY Repairs: By providing clear and user-friendly instructions, iFixit enables individuals with varying levels of technical expertise to perform do-it-yourself (DIY) repairs. This not only saves money but also gives users a sense of accomplishment for successfully fixing their devices.

Community Collaboration: iFixit encourages community collaboration, allowing users to contribute to the repair guides and share their own repair experiences. This fosters a sense of community and creates a collective knowledge base for repair enthusiasts.

Tools and Parts: The website also offers a marketplace where users can purchase specialized tools and replacement parts needed for their repairs. This makes it convenient for users to find the right components and tools for specific devices.

Support for Sustainable Practices: By promoting repairability, iFixit advocates for sustainable practices in consumer electronics. Repairing devices instead of discarding them helps reduce electronic waste and contributes to a more environmentally friendly approach to technology consumption.

Educational Resource: iFixit serves as an educational resource for individuals interested in understanding how electronics work and how to troubleshoot and repair common issues. It empowers users to become more informed and responsible consumers.

Tech Community Engagement: The iFixit website hosts a vibrant tech community with forums and discussion boards where users can seek help, share knowledge, and engage with other tech enthusiasts.

Advocacy for Right to Repair: iFixit is actively involved in the Right to Repair movement, advocating for consumer rights to repair their own devices and access repair information and spare parts from manufacturers.

Device Teardowns: iFixit is renowned for its thorough and detailed teardowns of the latest gadgets and electronic devices. These teardowns provide insights into the internal components and design of devices, which can be valuable for tech enthusiasts and industry professionals.

Overall, iFixit.com is a valuable resource for anyone seeking to repair their electronic devices, learn more about electronics, and promote sustainable and responsible consumer practices. Whether you're a seasoned repair expert or a beginner, iFixit's repair guides and community can be incredibly helpful in extending the lifespan of your devices and reducing electronic waste.

7... kumospace.com

Kumospace.com is an online platform designed to create virtual spaces for interactive gatherings, events, meetings, and social interactions. It provides a shared virtual environment where users can connect with others, collaborate, and engage in real-time. Here are some key points highlighting the potential usefulness of Kumospace.com:

Virtual Events and Meetings: Kumospace allows individuals and organizations to host virtual events, conferences, workshops, and meetings. It offers a unique and interactive space for participants to gather, communicate, and collaborate, regardless of their physical location.

Customizable Spaces: Users can customize their virtual spaces on Kumospace to reflect their branding, preferences, and event themes. This flexibility enables hosts to create immersive and engaging environments tailored to their specific needs.

Interactive Avatars: In Kumospace, participants are represented by avatars that can move around the virtual space and interact with each other. This adds a sense of presence and human interaction, making the virtual experience more engaging and enjoyable.

Proximity-Based Audio: The platform uses proximity-based audio, meaning that avatars can hear each other's conversations when they are close, creating a more natural and immersive communication experience.

Networking Opportunities: Kumospace facilitates networking opportunities, allowing participants to interact with one another in a casual and social setting. This can be particularly valuable for events or conferences where networking plays a crucial role.

Collaborative Tools: The platform may offer built-in collaborative tools like shared whiteboards, document sharing, and screen sharing, enhancing the ability to work together on projects or presentations.

Accessibility and Inclusivity: Virtual events on Kumospace can be accessible to a global audience, removing geographical barriers. Additionally, the platform may offer features that accommodate individuals with different accessibility needs.

Ease of Use: Kumospace aims to be user-friendly and easy to navigate, making it accessible to a broad range of users, including those who might not have extensive technical expertise.

It's essential to note that platforms like Kumospace may evolve over time, and new features or changes may have been introduced since my last update. For the latest and most accurate information about Kumospace.com and its offerings, I recommend visiting the official website or conducting further research to assess its current usefulness and capabilities.

8... Site.google.com

Site.google.com, also known as Google Sites, is a website creation tool provided by Google. It allows users to create and publish simple websites quickly and easily, without the need for extensive technical knowledge or coding skills. Here are some ways in which site.google.com can be useful:

User-Friendly Interface: Google Sites offers an intuitive and user-friendly interface that makes it easy for individuals, teams, or businesses to create websites without the complexity of traditional website development.

No Coding Required: Users can build websites using a drag-and-drop approach, meaning no coding or programming knowledge is necessary. This accessibility enables a broader range of people to create their own websites.

Integration with Google Workspace: Google Sites seamlessly integrates with other Google Workspace tools, such as Google Drive, Google Docs, and Google Calendar. This makes it convenient for users to embed and share various types of content on their websites.

Collaborative Editing: Multiple users can collaborate on the same Google Site simultaneously, allowing teams or groups to work together on website creation and updates.

Customization Options: While Google Sites is generally known for its simplicity, it does offer some customization options, allowing users to personalize their websites with themes, colors, and layouts.

Responsive Design: Google Sites automatically optimizes websites for various devices, ensuring that they are mobile-friendly and can be accessed on smartphones, tablets, and desktops.

Security and Reliability: As a Google service, Google Sites benefits from Google's robust security infrastructure and reliable hosting, ensuring that websites are secure and accessible to users.

Versatile Use Cases: Google Sites can be used for various purposes, such as creating personal portfolios, small business websites, project documentation, internal team pages, event websites, and more.

Low Cost: For individuals and small businesses on a budget, Google Sites can be a cost-effective solution as it's available for free with a Google account.

However, it's important to note that Google Sites may have some limitations compared to more advanced website creation platforms. For more complex or feature-rich websites, users may find Google Sites less suitable, and they might prefer other website builders that offer more extensive customization and functionality options.

Ultimately, the usefulness of site.google.com depends on the specific needs and requirements of the user or organization. It's best to evaluate the features and capabilities of Google Sites against the intended purpose of the website before deciding whether it's the right tool for the job.

9... Studypool.com

Studypool.com is an online platform that connects students seeking academic help with tutors and experts who can provide assistance with various subjects and homework assignments. It operates as a marketplace for academic help and tutoring. Here are some ways in which Studypool.com may be considered useful:

Academic Support: Studypool.com provides students with a platform to get academic support for their homework, assignments, and studies. Students can seek help from tutors or experts who have expertise in the subject areas they are struggling with.

Wide Range of Subjects: The platform covers a broad range of subjects and academic disciplines, making it a convenient one-stop destination for students seeking assistance in different areas of study.

Access to Experts: Studypool.com allows students to connect with tutors and experts from various backgrounds, including teachers, professionals, and subject matter experts. This access can provide valuable insights and explanations to help students understand challenging concepts.

Flexible Assistance: Students can ask questions or post specific assignments on Studypool.com, and tutors can bid on the tasks they are interested in helping with. This flexibility allows students to choose the best tutor based on their expertise and bid.

24/7 Availability: Studypool.com operates around the clock, making academic help accessible at any time, especially for students in different time zones or with urgent needs.

Diverse Learning Resources: In addition to direct tutoring, the platform may also offer study guides, video lessons, and other learning resources that can supplement students' understanding of the subject matter.

However, it's essential to consider potential concerns or challenges associated with using such platforms:

Academic Integrity: Students should be mindful of maintaining academic integrity when seeking help on Studypool.com or any similar platform. They should ensure that they use the assistance received appropriately and ethically, avoiding plagiarism or cheating.

Quality Control: The quality of assistance on platforms like Studypool.com can vary based on individual tutors and experts. It's crucial for students to verify the credentials and expertise of the tutors they choose to work with.

Cost Consideration: While some assistance on the platform may be free, more comprehensive help from qualified experts may come at a cost. Students should be mindful of their budget and weigh the value of the assistance they receive.

Subject Coverage: While Studypool.com covers a wide range of subjects, the availability of tutors and experts may vary across different disciplines.

As with any online service, users should exercise caution and research thoroughly before using Studypool.com or any other academic assistance platform. Reading reviews and understanding the terms and conditions of the platform can help students make informed decisions about its usefulness and suitability for their academic needs.

10...Voice.ai

"voice.ai" is a generic term that could refer to various companies, products, or services related to voice technology and artificial intelligence. Without specific context or information about a particular company or platform named "voice.ai," I cannot provide a detailed assessment of its usefulness or capabilities.

However, in general, voice AI technologies and applications have become increasingly prevalent and useful in various domains. Some common applications of voice AI include:

Virtual Assistants: Voice AI powers virtual assistant applications like Apple's Siri, Amazon's Alexa, Google Assistant, and others. These assistants can perform tasks, answer questions, and provide information through natural language voice commands.
Voice Recognition and Transcription: Voice AI technology is used to convert spoken language into written text, enabling automated transcription services, voice-controlled interfaces, and speech-to-text applications.
Voice Search and Navigation: Voice AI enables voice-activated search capabilities, making it easier for users to find information, products, or services online using their voice.
Voice Analytics: In some contexts, voice AI is used to analyze and understand voice patterns for insights into emotions, sentiment, or other relevant data.
Language Learning and Pronunciation: Voice AI can be employed in language learning platforms to provide feedback on pronunciation and language proficiency.
Voice Authentication and Security: Voice AI can be used for voice biometrics and authentication, enhancing security measures in various applications.
Accessibility: Voice AI technology plays a crucial role in making digital content and services accessible to people with visual or motor impairments.

It's important to note that the usefulness and effectiveness of a specific "voice.ai" platform or product will depend on its features, accuracy, user interface, and intended application. If you are interested in a particular voice AI service or platform, I recommend visiting their official website or conducting further research to assess its capabilities and determine its potential usefulness for your specific needs.

11... Unscreen.com

"Unscreen.com" is a website that offers an AI-powered tool for removing the background from videos and GIFs. It uses artificial intelligence and machine learning algorithms to automatically detect and eliminate the background, allowing users to create videos or GIFs with transparent backgrounds, often referred to as "green screen" or "chroma key" effects. Here are some key points about Unscreen.com and its potential usefulness:

Background Removal for Videos and GIFs: Unscreen.com specializes in removing backgrounds from videos and GIFs. This feature can be helpful for content creators, video editors, and social media users who want to add custom backgrounds or create visually appealing content without distracting backgrounds.

User-Friendly Interface: The platform aims to be user-friendly and straightforward, making it accessible to individuals with varying levels of video editing experience. Users can upload their videos or GIFs, and the AI-powered tool takes care of the background removal process.

Time-Saving Solution: Traditionally, removing backgrounds from videos or GIFs required complex editing software and considerable manual effort. Unscreen.com's automated process can save users time and effort in achieving the desired results.

Green Screen Replacement: Unscreen.com can be particularly useful for creators who don't have access to a physical green screen setup. The tool allows them to achieve similar effects without the need for specialized equipment.

Creative Content Creation: By removing backgrounds, users can add creative and custom backgrounds to their videos or GIFs, making their content more engaging and visually appealing.

Transparent Backgrounds for Social Media: Transparent background videos or GIFs are useful for various social media platforms, where eye-catching visuals can help content stand out in feeds.

Integration with Other Editing Software: After using Unscreen.com to remove backgrounds, users can integrate the resulting videos or GIFs into other video editing software or platforms for further enhancements and adjustments.

Personal and Commercial Use: Depending on the platform's terms of service, users may be able to use the edited videos or GIFs for personal projects or even commercial purposes.

As with any online service, it's essential to be mindful of the platform's terms of use, privacy policies, and any associated costs or limitations. For the latest and most accurate information about Unscreen.com and its features, I recommend visiting the official website or reading user reviews to gauge its usefulness and reliability.

12...flowcv.com

"flowcv.com" is a website that offers a platform for creating professional and visually appealing resumes, also known as CVs (Curriculum Vitae). It aims to help job seekers and professionals design impressive resumes that stand out to potential employers. Here are some key points about FlowCV and its potential usefulness:

Easy Resume Creation: FlowCV provides a user-friendly interface that allows individuals to create resumes easily and efficiently. It offers customizable templates and formatting options to tailor the resume to the user's specific needs and preferences.

Visual Appeal: The platform focuses on creating visually appealing resumes with a modern design. By using attractive templates and layouts, FlowCV helps users present their skills and experiences in an aesthetically pleasing manner.

Professional Templates: FlowCV likely offers a range of professional templates for various industries and career levels. This can be particularly helpful for individuals who want a polished and well-structured resume without the need for extensive design skills.

Online Resume Hosting: FlowCV may offer the option to host resumes online, allowing users to share their CVs via a personalized URL. This feature can make it easier for job seekers to share their credentials with potential employers or colleagues.

Version Control: Some resume builders, including FlowCV, may provide version control, enabling users to keep track of different resume versions tailored to specific job applications or opportunities.

Export Options: FlowCV likely allows users to export their resumes in various formats, such as PDF or Word, making it convenient to download and print or attach the resume to job applications.

Accessibility and Device Compatibility: Being an online platform, FlowCV can be accessed from any device with an internet connection, offering flexibility to users who want to update or access their resumes on the go.

Privacy and Security: Resume builders often prioritize data privacy and security. Users should review the platform's privacy policy and terms of service to understand how their personal information is handled.

As with any resume-building platform, it's essential to consider whether FlowCV's features and templates align with your specific resume needs and the industries you are targeting.

Additionally, users should verify the current status and offerings of "flowcv.com" by visiting the website directly or reading recent reviews and testimonials.

13... Creatorset.com

Content creation platforms usually offer a variety of tools, resources, and community support for individuals interested in producing their own content, such as videos, blogs, podcasts, and more. These tools might include editing software, graphics generators, SEO helpers, community forums, and advice or tutorials on successful content creation.

To understand the usefulness of this particular site, I'd recommend checking it out directly to see the services it provides, reading user reviews, and comparing it with other similar platforms to see if it meets your specific needs.

14...Vlipsy.com

Vlipsy is a platform that allows users to search for and share video clips, often used as reactions, similar to how GIFs are used. These video clips, or "Vlips," can be used in various social media platforms and messaging apps. Users can also upload their own clips, contributing to the searchable database.

The usefulness of Vlipsy would depend on your specific needs. If you frequently communicate on platforms that support this kind of content and enjoy using multimedia to express yourself, you might find Vlipsy to be a valuable resource. It allows for more dynamic and engaging communication compared to text-only messaging. However, it's worth noting that like any online platform, the content available will vary in quality and relevance.

15... Fireflies.ai

Fireflies.ai is a tool that offers automated note-taking for meetings. It's designed to integrate with various popular meeting platforms such as Zoom, Google Meet, and Microsoft Teams.

The platform uses artificial intelligence to transcribe and capture action items from meetings, saving time and effort for participants who would otherwise need to manually take notes. It can be particularly useful for businesses and teams that have frequent meetings and need a way to efficiently document important points and follow-up actions.

Key features of Fireflies.ai generally include:

1. Transcription: The AI can transcribe meetings in real-time, turning spoken words into written text.
2. Action Items: The tool can identify and highlight key tasks or actions discussed during the meeting.
3. Search Functionality: Users can search through past meetings for specific topics, phrases, or keywords.
4. Integration: Fireflies.ai can integrate with various other tools like CRM software, project management apps, and more.

Keep in mind that you should review the site's privacy and data handling policies to ensure they align with your or your organization's standards. Also, the specific features and functionality might have been updated or changed since my last training cut-off.

16…000tube.com

is a free online YouTube video downloader that allows users to download videos from YouTube instantly and easily. Simply paste a YouTube link in the textbox above and download your favorite videos right away.

With this YouTube downloader tool, you can download YouTube videos in HD quality without having to install any additional software or browser extensions. The tool is 100% online and free to use.

We've built this online video tool to allow teachers and educators to save videos for use in the classroom, journalists who want to keep a copy of important videos before they're removed from the platform, and others who wish to download YouTube videos that are copyright-free for offline use.

It is the safest and the best alternative to Y2Mate, SaveFrom, BTClod, QDownloader, BitDownloader, X2Mate, 4K Video Downloader, 8Downloader, and other websites that are filled with malicious ads.

Here are the steps.

1. Go to YouTube's website and open the video that you want to download.

2. Copy the video's link from your browser's address bar.

3. Paste the link into the search box on 10Downloader, such as the one at the top of this page.

4. 10Downloader will automatically begin searching for the video. It will display the results within a few seconds.

5. Determine the video resolution that you want to save, then right-click on the Download button and select the "Save", "Save As", or "Save Link As" option. The naming will vary depending on the browser that you use.

6. The YouTube video will begin to download to your computer and will be saved to your default or the selected downloads folder.

17...reimaginehome.ai

Redesign any space to match your vision, or let this AI show you inspiring designs in seconds.

This AI redesigns any space through evaluating architectural elements, detecting room type, understanding preferred design styles and adhering to your color preferences & text instructions.

This AI re-designs furnished spaces by automatically considering all architectural elements, such as doors and walls, as well as furniture pieces, ranging from beds to paintings.

This AI automatically re-designs exterior spaces and patios, taking into account architectural elements such as lawns, backyards, pools and outdoor furniture/appliances – from benches to barbeque setups.

design assistant
social media assistant
Increase conversions & improve creatives on the fly. Get creative data in seconds with Predict

Improve Creative Performance with Attention Prediction

Create high-converting creatives

Understand how your customers respond to your creatives

Improve performance with data-driven design
Maximize creative impact
Measure attention and engagement at a click of a button. Ensure that your creatives deliver, without burning budget on A/B testing.

With Predict you can:
Optimize creatives & assets, all the way from ads to websites

Increase conversions with more powerful images & videos

Take the guesswork out of your design processes

Boost brand awareness

Draw attention to your ads and drive brand awareness and activation with high ROAS.

Drive in-store & online sales

Improve sales & increase brand strength with enticing packaging & in-store designs.

Improve user engagement

Optimize your website & online store for more conversions and lower cart abandonment.

video editing
video generator
personalized videos
A VIRTUAL STUDIO THAT MAKES VIDEO PRODUCTION STUPIDLY SIMPLE
Create Thought Leadership videos and builds trust and credibility
Build a loyal client base with product announcements, news & updates
Stand out and captivate your audience with powerful Marketing Videos
Invite guests, experts and your team for a more engaging content
Educate your audience with Tutorials, and Explainer videos
Create Interviews, testimonials and scale your Community Reach

20...embedditor.ai

Optimize the relevance of the content you get back from a vector database, intelligently splitting or merging the content based on its structure and adding void or hidden tokens, making chunks even more semantically coherent.

Get better security

Get the full control over your data, effortlessly deploying Embedditor locally on your PC or in your dedicated enterprise cloud or on-premises environment.

Reduce your costs

Applying Embedditor advanced cleansing techniques to filter out from embedding irrelevant tokens like stop-words, punctuations, and low-relevant frequently words, you can save up to 40% on the cost of embedding and vector storage while getting better search results.

21...caspa.ai

Create in minutesRealistic human models. Your own products.

Cointains

Algorithm Designer

A tool to write the most efficient algorithm to do a given task

SpeechWriter

A tool for crafting powerful speeches quickly and easily

Keyword Generator

A tool to quickly generate relevant keywords for any topic or subject.

Travel Guide

A chatbot that can act as your personal travel guide

ComedianGPT

A tool for easily writing jokes

Fitness Coach

A personal AI chatbot that provides tailored physical training plans

C Code Writer

A tool for writing C code to perform a given task or set of tasks.

Programming Language Conversion Tool

A powerful tool for converting code from one programming language to another

Go Code Writing Tool

A tool to write Go code to perform a given task.

Script-Writing Tool

A tool for quickly and easily writing scripts for any purpose.

StoryWriter

A tool to help you write stories quickly and easily,

And many more....

23…gptgo.ai

GPTGO still returns search results as usual, but adds a chatGPT query feature, so the results will also include ChatGPT answers.
life assistant
search engine

Create better LinkedIn content
10x faster with AI
Get content ideas and inspiration, write incredible hooks and optimise your posts' formatting and schedule content. All in one place
Export entire searches, lead lists, or projects from LinkedIn.

Engage Your Audience: Create attention-grabbing hooks and posts that captivate your LinkedIn audience.

Save Time and Effort: Generate compelling post ideas effortlessly, eliminating writer's block and saving you valuable time.

Maximise Reach: Tap into the power of AI to identify viral trends and create posts that resonate with your target audience, boosting your reach and visibility.
Save time and ensure consistency on your posts.

See how your LinkedIn posts will appear before sharing them. Ensure they look great and make a positive impression on your network.

Avoid embarrassing errors by previewing your posts. Spot typos, grammar issues, or formatting glitches before you hit the publish button.

Preview and perfect the layout, choose eye-catching visuals, and craft compelling wording that grabs attention and boosts engagement.

25…Namelix

Business Name Generator
generate a short, brandable business name using artificial intelligence
Get name ideas
Namelix generates short, catchy names with a state of the art language model
Filter results
Decide whether you prioritize a shorter name, having a specific keyword or domain extension
Save your names
Our algorithm learns from the names you like, giving you better recommendations over time
For new businesses, naming options can seem quite limited. Short domains are very expensive, yet longer multi-word names don't inspire confidence.

In 2023 many startups are choosing a short, branded name - a name that's unique, memorable and affordable.
Most business name generators combine dictionary words to make longer names.

Namelix generates short, branded names that are relevant to your business idea. When you save a name, the algorithm learns your preferences and gives you better recommendations over time.

AlternativeTo is a website that offers recommendations for software alternatives. Users can search for a software that they know and love (or hate) and the site will provide alternatives that other users have suggested for similar functionality. The alternatives are ranked by user endorsements.

This can be a useful tool if you're looking for a different software solution but you're not sure what options are out there. It can help you find lesser-known but well-liked software, free alternatives to paid solutions, or just give you ideas for tools that serve a similar purpose to ones you're already familiar with.

As with all user-generated content, it's a good idea to do your own research and make sure any software you choose is safe and reliable. Also, keep in mind that the most popular options aren't always the best for every person or every use case, so consider your specific needs as you explore.

Translate and add subtitles to any video
Adding subtitles or closed captions to a video not only makes your content more accessible but also improves viewer engagement. Here are some steps on how to translate and add subtitles to any video:

1. **Transcription**: The first step is to transcribe your video. If the video is not in your native language or the language you're comfortable with, use a translation service to translate the dialogue into the desired language. You can manually transcribe the video or use automated transcription services like Descript, Rev, or online AI tools.

2. **Timing**: Once you have the transcript, you need to time the subtitles to match the dialogue in the video. This can be done manually using video editing software, or with the help of online tools like Aegisub that help synchronize the text with the video.

3. **Formatting and Encoding**: After timing the subtitles, format them to ensure they're easily readable. This involves choosing a good font, size, and color. Finally, encode the subtitles into the video. Some video players require subtitles to be in a specific file format like .SRT or .SUB.

4. **Embedding Subtitles**: Depending on where you're hosting the video, the process for adding subtitles will vary. Most online platforms like YouTube, Vimeo, and Facebook have built-in tools that allow you to upload a subtitle file directly.

5. **Review and Edit**: It's crucial to review the subtitled video for any errors in translation or timing. Be sure to correct these errors before finalizing the video.

6. **Machine Learning Tools**: You can also use advanced AI-based tools like Google's AutoML, AWS Transcribe, or Microsoft Azure's Video Indexer, which can automatically transcribe and translate the spoken language in the video.

Remember, accurate translation and synchronization of subtitles are critical to ensure the message of the video is conveyed correctly.

Trasform your mic to better quality
Improving the audio quality of your microphone can make a significant difference in the clarity and professionalism of your audio recordings or broadcasts. Here are a few steps you can take:

1. **Positioning**: Position the microphone close to your mouth but slightly to the side to avoid harsh "p" and "b" sounds. Also, avoid moving around too much to maintain consistent audio levels.

2. **Use a Pop Filter**: This is a screen that is placed between you and the microphone. It reduces or eliminates the popping sounds that are caused by the mechanical impact of fast-moving air on the microphone during recorded speech.

3. **Acoustic Treatment**: Reduce background noise and echo by recording in a quiet, carpeted room with lots of soft furnishings. You can also use professional foam panels for better sound absorption.

4. **Use a High-Quality Microphone**: USB microphones are convenient and often good enough for most people. However, if you're looking for top-notch audio quality, consider using a professional XLR microphone with an audio interface.

5. **Gain Setting**: Set the gain level correctly. If it's too high, the audio will distort; if it's too low, you will hear background noise.

6. **Software Enhancement**: Use audio editing software to improve the sound quality. Programs like Audacity (free) or Adobe Audition (paid) can be used to reduce background noise, equalize the sound, and make your voice clearer.

Remember, each microphone and recording situation is unique, so you might need to experiment a bit to find out what works best for you.

29.....Futurepedia.io

One website combine all ai websites
A platform that combines all AI-related websites or resources into one place does not currently exist, as of my knowledge cutoff in September 2021. AI is a vast field with numerous subdomains and applications, which makes it challenging to encapsulate every AI-related website under one umbrella. However, there are sites that aggregate AI tools, services, and resources.

Here are some points on this topic:

1. **AI directories**: Websites like AI Directory or AI Stack are platforms where AI-related tools, apps, and services are listed and categorized. These directories are designed to help people discover and compare various AI offerings.

2. **AI News and Research**: Websites like Arxiv, MIT Technology Review, or AI Topics by AAAI offer a compilation of recent research, news, and articles related to AI.

3. **AI Learning Resources**: Sites like Coursera, edX, and Kaggle provide a wide range of AI and machine learning courses, datasets, and competitions.

4. **Open Source AI**: Platforms like GitHub are abundant with AI-related projects, libraries, and tools which are shared and developed collaboratively.

5. **Marketplaces**: Some cloud platforms offer marketplaces where you can access and use pre-trained AI models. Examples include AWS Marketplace for Machine Learning and Google Cloud AI Hub.

When using such websites, it's crucial to ensure that the source of the AI tool or service is reliable and that it respects user privacy and data handling standards. As with any tool, consider your specific requirements and constraints when choosing an AI service or resource.

30...krunker.io

Krunker.io,is a popular online first-person shooter game. It's known for its fast-paced gameplay and pixel-style graphics.

Here are some key features:

1. **Browser-Based**: Krunker.io is played directly in your web browser, so there's no need to download any software to play. This makes it easily accessible on most computers.

2. **Multiplayer**: It's a multiplayer game where you compete against other players from around the world in various modes such as Free-For-All, Team Deathmatch, and more.

3. **Character Classes**: Krunker.io offers a variety of character classes, each with unique weapons and abilities, giving the player a range of styles to play with.

4. **Customization and Community**: The game allows for a significant amount of customization, including custom maps and mods. It also has a robust community creating and sharing content.

5. **Free to Play**: The game is free to play, though there are options to purchase in-game items and cosmetics.

As with any online game, remember to be mindful of online safety, such as not sharing personal information and being respectful to other players.

"Build a little town endlessly" likely refers to a genre of games known as "endless builders" or "idle city builders." These games focus on the continuous construction and expansion of a city or town, often without a specific end goal, hence the "endlessly".

Here are some points to note:

1. **Gameplay**: Players usually start with a small piece of land and gradually add buildings, improve infrastructure, and attract citizens to grow their town. Gameplay often involves managing resources, planning strategies for growth, and making decisions that impact the development of the town.

2. **Progression**: In these games, progression is often marked by the size and complexity of your town or city, and the number of citizens it can support. Some games offer challenges or objectives to guide your development.

3. **Idle Mechanic**: Many of these games feature an 'idle' mechanic where your city continues to grow and generate resources even when you're not actively playing. This can add an element of strategy as you plan for long-term growth.

4. **Examples**: Games like SimCity BuildIt, Pocket City, or Townsmen can be considered part of this genre.

5. **Accessibility**: These games are typically easy to pick up and play and can be enjoyed by players of all ages and skill levels.

As with any game, the enjoyment comes from engaging gameplay, a sense of progress, and the satisfaction of building and managing your own town or city. These games can be a creative outlet and a fun way to pass time.

32...Meboom.ai

Generate Stunnig Avatars with Meboom.ai

1.   AI-Based Avatars: AI can be used to create unique and customizable avatars. It can generate a diverse range of facial features, hairstyles, clothing, and more.

2.   Customization: These platforms usually allow a high degree of customization, enabling users to create avatars that align with their preferences.

3.   Applications: Such avatars can be used in various applications, including social media profiles, gaming, virtual reality environments, or any other platform where a user might want a digital representation of themselves.

4.   Ease of Use: AI-based avatar generators are typically designed to be user-friendly, often requiring little more than a few clicks to generate a result.

5.   Privacy: As with any AI tool, especially one that may involve user images or personal characteristics, it's important to review the platform's privacy policy and data handling procedures.

33...edx.org

EdX.org is a massive open online course (MOOC) provider that offers university-level courses in a wide range of disciplines. It's a nonprofit organization started by Harvard University and MIT in 2012.

Here are some key features and benefits of edX:

1. **Wide Range of Courses**: EdX offers over 2000 online courses from top institutions around the world in subjects like computer science, business, engineering, data science, languages, and more.

2. **High-Quality Content**: The courses are created by top universities and institutions, ensuring high-quality content and teaching.

3. **Flexible Learning**: Most courses on edX can be taken at your own pace, making it a great option for people who want to learn while balancing other commitments.

4. **Free to Audit**: Most courses on edX can be audited for free. This means you can access the course materials and learn without paying, but you won't receive a certificate upon completion. If you want a certificate, you can opt to pay for the verified track.

5. **MicroMasters and Professional Certificates**: EdX also offers MicroMasters programs and professional certificates for learners who want to earn a credential for career or academic advancement.

6. **Financial Assistance**: EdX offers financial assistance to learners who demonstrate need, allowing them to earn verified certificates at a reduced cost.

Remember, like with any online learning platform, the value you get from edX will depend on your dedication to the course, your active participation, and how you apply what you learn.